John Be
CITY OF LONDON
CHURCHES

Before the Fire of London in 1666 there were ninety-seven parish churches within the walls of the City of London. Fifty-one were rebuilt by Sir Christopher Wren and new ones were built in the 18th and 19th centuries. Today a mere thirty-nine survive and each one is worthy of a visit.

ABOVE: *St Bride's, Fleet Street.*

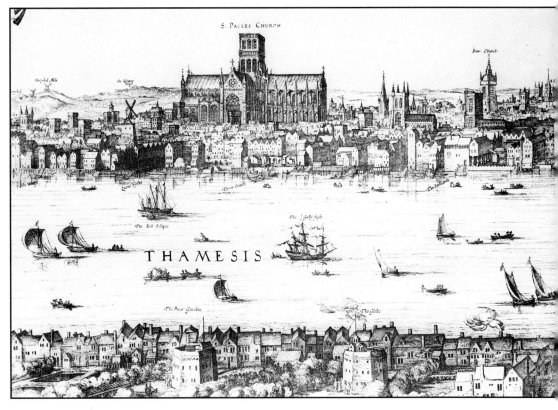

S. PAVLES CHVRCH

THAMESIS

ABOVE: *Vischer's engraving of 1616 shows the City of London from Southwark. The towers and spires of some forty medieval churches can be counted.*

The Medieval City of London

The walled medieval City of London had only one bridge, London Bridge, and this, with its narrow arches, acted as a sluice. Above the bridge, the Thames was slower flowing than it is now, and wider, slopping over the Surrey marshes and crowded with little boats. Queenhithe, the old City harbour, above the bridge, may still be seen. St Paul's Cathedral was founded in the 7th century and before it was burnt in 1666 had grown to be the longest cathedral in Europe. It dominated the City.

Within the City walls there were ninety-seven parish churches before the Fire. The oldest were Saxon in origin and most had Norman remains. Some are very small, like the recently reopened St Ethelburga, Bishopsgate. Others were big monastic buildings like the Augustinian priory of St Bartholomew whose

choir and transepts still survive. Every timbered, crowded house in the narrow alleys must have been within sound of a church bell. The older parish churches gave birth to others. For instance, St Mary Aldermary had four St Mary churches formed from it. The most famous of these is St Mary-le-Bow. Some had stone towers with little wooden turrets such as may be seen on country church towers in Hertfordshire. Some only had turrets. Others were rich enough to afford a spire. All had gilded vanes. Inside they had painted walls, stained glass and screened chapels whose lights, furnishing and priests were often paid for by the medieval trade guilds which survive in the City today and are still connected with their parish churches. After the Fire thirty-five churches were not rebuilt. Many of the sites

have been built over but often the churchyards survive.

The Fire of London in 1666 destroyed St Paul's and the whole City except its eastern and north-eastern edges. The citizens first set about rebuilding their houses and shops in brick this time, instead of timber. Sir Christopher Wren, a high churchman, a young professor at Oxford, a mathematician, astronomer and model-maker, was appointed by his friend Charles II as Surveyor-General to the King's works with an office in Scotland Yard. Wren, the Bishop of London and the Archbishop of Canterbury were the committee for rebuilding the City churches.

The first thing to do was to rebuild the bodies of the churches and Wren was responsible for fifty-one of them.

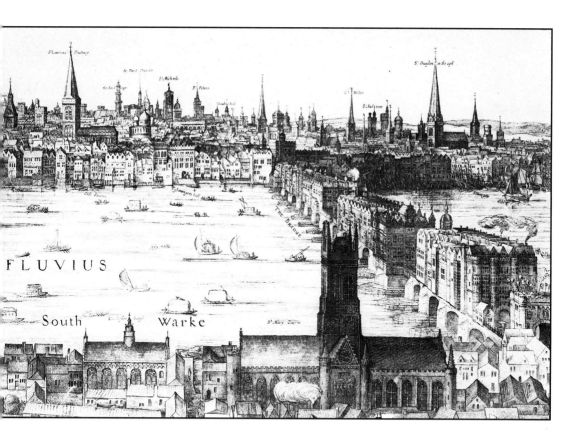

FLUVIUS

South Warke

Wren – A Man of the Renaissance

Some of the churches he left to his surveyors. The woodwork and furnishings were contracted for by the parishioners with various local craftsmen, which accounts for the different styles and quality of carving and ironwork. The fabrics were paid for by parochial subscription and also by the State by a tax on coal. As the idea of a domed cathedral to replace St Paul's grew in Wren's mind, so the skyline of the City became important to him and he added towers, spires and steeples to the churches in white Portland stone or lead, to enhance the effect of his great cathedral whose first storey, drum and dome sailed over the red brick houses and dominated the clustering churches within the City.

Wren never went beyond Paris in his travels where he studied French methods of building. He was a man of the Renaissance but no high-handed theoriser. His City churches,

in their plans, show every aspect of the church for which they were built. All had prominent font and altar. The latter had carved and painted altar-piece above. Thus were emphasised the two sacraments essential to salvation in the Catholic Church, baptism and Holy Communion. All had a prominent pulpit in the nave for preaching the Word and seats ranged within hearing distance. Thereafter they had nothing in common. Some were rebuilt with nave, aisles and chancel screen on the medieval plan. Others were cross-shaped with a central dome, others were wholly domed, some had only one aisle and some were oblong and un-aisled. All had clear glass windows so as to show the wood carving, painted altar-pieces and ironwork. Very often Wren tried to reproduce in his own style the church that had been there before the Fire. He took particular trouble

with the steeple of St Mary-le-Bow and the spire of St Dunstan-in-the-East. Sometimes he even went so far as to rebuild in Gothic.

Wren's cheerful genius pervades the whole City even today when his buildings have been dwarfed by boring office slabs and the famous skyline to which he gave such thought obliterated. His churches were light, varied and happy, and seem to reflect the kind, detached smile we see on the face of his bust in the Ashmolean Museum, Oxford.

Several City churches were rebuilt by their parishioners in the 18th century. The mathematical precision of Hawksmoor at St Mary Woolnoth, the light elegance of George Dance Junior at All Hallows-on-the-Wall and his imitator at St Botolphs Aldersgate are all in a different world from Wren. The rebuilding of old churches which had escaped the Fire and even, in the

Sir Christopher Wren, astronomer, mathematician, and architect. In the background of the painting is St Paul's Cathedral, his crowning glory. Following the Fire of London in 1666, Wren was responsible for rebuilding fifty-one City of London churches, each one a masterpiece. Many were destroyed in Victorian times and in the 1940 bombing.

1830s, the building of new churches on the overcrowded western banks of the Fleet river, continued because the City was residential until the coming of railways. The walls and medieval gates remained until 1760. Citizens such as John Gilpin went on living over their places of business. Different districts were associated with particular trades. For instance, Crooked Lane was noted for the manufacture of fishing tackle, bird-cages and hand mills, and even today bankers, fishmongers, printers, butchers, poulterers and brokers have their special districts.

The churches maintained parish schools until the last century, and many school buildings survive. The richer sort of citizen moved out into Middlesex, Essex and Hertfordshire in the 18th century and the middling sort to the new estates round Highbury and Islington in the late Georgian era. The smaller hand trades continued in City alleys, fighting a losing battle with mass production in Birmingham and the North. A few such trades survive in the northern and eastern wards. Citizens who had moved out maintained a connection with the parish of their ancestors by coming in for Sunday worship. One such is described as 'A City Personage' in the chapter on the City churches in Charles Dickens' *The Uncommercial Traveller.*

The great change to the City and its churches came in the middle of the 19th century. Britannia ruled the waves and the commercial prosperity of England was London and the heart of London was the City. Land values soared and offices in the City were more needed than houses. The resident population sank to the 6,000 it is today. Railways, first steam and then electric, drew in and out their loads of office workers. Lord Mayors came from Lewisham instead of Cheapside and their family vaults are in Norwood and other London cemeteries. In the 1860s the restrictions on building heights were raised and many of Wren's steeples were obscured by Victorian and Edwardian office blocks. Owing to the increased value of land in the City, many of Wren's churches were sold by successive bishops of London and the money used for building churches in the new suburbs – a form of simony which has never paid dividends. Between 1782 and 1939 twenty-six City churches were destroyed, nineteen of them Wren's. Late Georgian church building in the City favoured the new craze for Gothic which started with George Dance Junior's ingenious Gothic octagon for St Bartholomew-the-Less. This Gothic, right up to St Dunstan-in-the-West by J. Shaw (1831), was really Georgian building with Gothic decoration. The serious medievalism of the mid-Victorians and the craze for surpliced choirs in stalls in the chancel, and for stained glass giving a dim religious light, made a double assault on the City churches from the 1850s onwards. First Wren's Classical style was regarded as pagan and this furnished an excuse for destroying so many of his churches. Clumsy attempts were made to give the rest 'Christian' furnishings. Medieval churches were regarded with sacred awe and severely scraped, tooled over and refurnished.

Almost all the City churches were damaged by German bombing in

1940 and several were totally destroyed. Eleven churches, seven of them Wren's, have not been rebuilt. In 1782 there were sixty-nine churches in the City. Today there are under forty. The Victorians destroyed several of Wren's masterpieces of which the greatest were St Antholin Watling Street and St Benet Fink and the sumptuous interior of St Mildred Poultry. The Germans deprived us of Wren's exquisite domed church of St Mildred Bread Street which had all its old woodwork and high pews. They certainly did us the favour of blowing out much bad Victorian glass. It has been sad to see that in almost all the Wren churches which have been restored since the bombing stained glass has been reintroduced for buildings never intended to contain it. Restorations have varied with the sensitivity of the architects employed. There is no doubt that it was wise of the Church of England to rebuild so much of its heritage in the City. As the noise and reek of diesel oil in the streets grow greater, and as the impersonal slabs of cellular offices rise higher into the sky, so do the churches which remain in the City of London today become more valuable to us. They maintain a human scale and still mark off the City from the rest of London, recalling lost lanes of little shops where clerks could spend their lunch hour.

Even today some of these lanes survive, scattered throughout the city, as do the livery company halls with their panelled wood and candle-light on carving, silver and ermine and red faces full of port wine. The City churches also reflect, by their variety, the varied quality of the City itself. One can hardly believe that St Botolph Aldgate, with its mission to the East End, is in the same city as the polished aldermanic splendour of St Lawrence Jewry, the Corporation church. There is a difference of atmosphere even in two of Wren's domed churches. St Stephen Walbrook with its forest of columns feels wide open to the streets, while St Mary Abchurch is sumptuous but intimate.

Apart from the old customs and connections with livery companies which make City of London churches different from other churches, they have this in common – that they are all increasingly used on weekdays, particularly those where the incumbent is to be found in the church.

This guide does not mention, for reasons of space, places of worship outside the Anglican communion. The Dutch church in Austin Friars was a medieval building entirely destroyed by the Germans and has been rebuilt in semi-Classical style. The Roman Catholic church of St Mary Moorfield, which survived the bombing, is a charming rebuilding (1902) by George Sherrin of an impressive Corinthian chapel built in 1820. The synagogue for Sephardi Jews in Bevis Marks also luckily escaped bombing. It was built in 1701 by a Quaker and has all its original woodwork and candelabra.

I am indebted to the inspiring book *Old London Churches* by Elizabeth and Wayland Young (Faber & Faber, 1956); and to Gerald Cobb's *Old London Churches* (B. T. Batsford, 3rd ed. 1948), as well as his admirable brief guide to the London City Churches published by the Corporation of London (2nd ed. 1962).

BELOW:
An 18th-century view of the spires of the City of London.

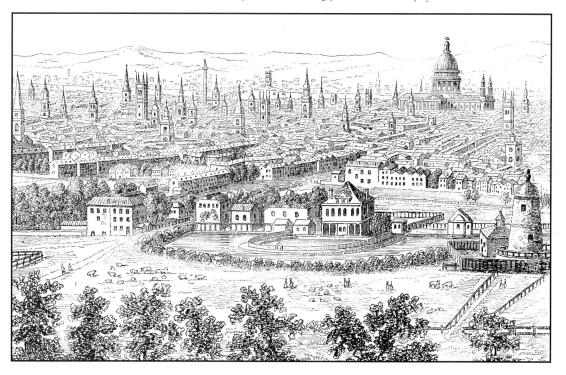

ALL HALLOWS-BY-THE-TOWER

(sometimes called All Hallows Barking)
pre Great Fire;
17th century, rebuilt 20th century.
GREAT TOWER STREET

The Great Fire of London started in Pudding Lane, a few hundred yards from the church. Through the efforts of Admiral Penn (father of William Penn, the founder of Pennsylvania), All Hallows survived, but in 1940 Hitler's bombs succeeded where the Great Fire failed and only the 17th-century brick tower (from which Pepys had watched the fire) and the walls remained. In 1948 a new foundation stone was laid by Her Majesty Queen Elizabeth the Queen Mother who attended the rededication service some nine years later. The vicar at the time was 'Tubby' Clayton, founder of Toc H (Talbot House), a society which continues the comradeship of the First World War.

The rest of the building is the post-war creation of the late Lord Mottistone, who finished it in 1957. He added the spire to the old brick tower, because bombing of the surrounding buildings had suddenly brought it into prominence from many viewpoints and it was made as a conscious addition to an empty bit of skyline. The church was founded in 675 by the Saxon Abbey of Barking, and an arch from the original church remains. Beneath the arch is a Roman pavement of about AD 45, with Saxon walling round it. The body of the church, with galleries, clerestoried nave and concrete barrel-roof, all in an airy Perpendicular style, is by Lord Mottistone. The pulpit is from Wren's church of St Swithin, London Stone, which was destroyed after being bombed in the last war.

The carved limewood font cover (1682), showing two cherubs struggling round hops and corn with a dove above, is one of the most exquisite bits of carving in any London church.

Next to the Tower of London, the church has received numerous beheaded bodies, including those of Thomas More, John Fisher and Archbishop William Laud. William Penn was baptised in the church and educated in the schoolroom, and John Quincy Adams, 6th President of the United States of America, was married here in 1797.

ALL HALLOWS-ON-THE-WALL

re-built 1765–7, George Dance Jnr.
LONDON WALL

The little Portland stone tower and cupola on the edge of London Wall welcome the walker from the west, after the Barbican. The church outside is an oblong whose brown brick south wall is treated with simple boldness. The interior is light, chaste, elegant and ingenious. The barrel-vaulted ceiling decorated in white and gold is lit on either side by a clerestory of wide semi-circular windows. It rises on fluted Ionic pilasters from a frieze. There is no cornice; a daring and deliberate breaking of the Classic convention of the time. The west end with its organ case and gallery is plain. The pulpit is approached from the vestry by stairs in the north wall, which is built on the old wall of the City. The painting over the altar is by Nathaniel Dance Holland, brother of the architect. Part of the old floors remains. The font is from St Mary Magdalene, Old Fish Street, by way of St Paul's and the organ came from Islington Parish Hall.

LEFT: *All Hallows-by-the-Tower. The famous diarist Samuel Pepys watched the Fire of London from the tower.*

ST ANDREW, HOLBORN
pre-Great Fire, rebuilt by Wren 1687.
HOLBORN CIRCUS

A large church for the City, it was originally designed to be seen from the Fleet River, where the east end and tower seem related. Portland stone on the tower at the west end is a later casing in the lower stages to the medieval tower as seen internally; it has complicated Classic windows and heavy cornice and pinnacles. Between the tower and slightly projecting east end, with domed vestries either side, are double rows of clear glass windows denoting a galleried church, and so the interior proves to be. Wren's scheme of square panelled wooden columns supporting the gallery fronts, from which rise round, Corinthian stone columns, has been used. The columns support groined gallery roofs and barrel vaulted nave ceiling.

The present interior was rebuilt in 1960 after the bombing of 1941 and the coloured and gilded plasterwork of the ceiling is a repetition of what was there before. The east window by Brian Thomas is an attempt to compensate for the loss of the superb 18th-century glass which used to be in all three east windows. There is a marble font and gilded organ case of great beauty. The organ given by Handel in 1750 to Foundling Hospital, is at the west end. The *trompe l'oeil* of a dove over the altar of the chapel, approached through the 15th-century stone arches of tower, is by Brian Thomas. The gilded altarpiece which surrounds it is from the ruined church of St Luke, Old Street, as are the delicately-wrought iron communion rails. The vicarage on the south side is a Gothic brick and stone enclave by S. S. Teulon.

BELOW LEFT: *The interior of All Hallows London Wall is light and elegant; the ceiling is of white and gold.*
BELOW RIGHT: *The refurbishment of St Andrew Holborn in 1960 included new stained glass by Brian Thomas in the east window.*

ST ANDREW UNDERSHAFT
pre-Great Fire.
LEADENHALL STREET

This church was badly affected by a bomb in 1992 and considerable effort has been made to completely restore the building.

Of all the Gothic churches in the City, this is the most stately, although the outside is unpromising. The tower, with its prominent newel stair turret, is Victorian on top and has a Renaissance entrance door and iron gates. The interior, rebuilt 1520–32, is tall East Anglian Gothic, with north and south aisle arcades of six bays and a shallow chancel. The nave roof, which is wooden and flat, was renewed in 1950 with the old bosses, but it still looks new and does not match the old wooden roofs of the aisles.

The original east window of golden and glorious 17th-century glass, showing English monarchs and heraldry, was moved to the west by the Victorians who put in the anaemic east window and moved the

splendid late 17th-century carved organ case to its present awkward position in the south-east corner. They also put in ugly tiled floors. The west window was destroyed in the bomb blast and has been replaced. But much 17th-century ironwork in the form of communion rail and swordrests survives along with the wall painting. The font is by Nicholas Stone and dates from before the Fire, as does the monument to John Stow, London's famous historian, with a quill pen in his hand.

ST ANDREW-BY-THE-WARDROBE
Wren 1685–95.
QUEEN VICTORIA STREET

A simple, dark red brick oblong with plain tower and double rows of clear glass windows. A rectory adjoins it, on the attractive St Andrew's Hill, and there are two little churchyards in the former St Ann's parish.

The church was completely gutted in the Blitz of 1940 and entirely renewed inside by Marshall Sisson so that it does not, as yet, look

old. The aisles are shut in and there is, consequently, an overwhelming effect of light, new woodwork. There are galleries all round and a screen below the west gallery. The ceiling of the whole church is very attractive. Over the aisles it has quadripartite vaulting and over the nave it is barrel-roofed and decorated with charming rough Renaissance plaster-work in the form of wreaths of fruit and flowers and semi-circles and spandrels of cherubs. There are candelabra in the nave.

ST ANNE AND ST AGNES
Wren 1676–87.
GRESHAM STREET

A refreshing red brick interlude in the modern mediocrity of Gresham Street. It has an entrance through the churchyard on the south with a small western tower crowned by a turret with a vane shaped in the letter A and round-headed windows under central pediments on the other three sides.

The inside is a surprise, with a

ABOVE LEFT: *The new-looking interior of St Andrew-by-the-Wardrobe.*
ABOVE RIGHT: *St Bartholomew-the-Great. The five medieval bells in the 17th-century tower form the oldest complete ring in London.*

low central dome supported on four Corinthian columns giving a cross plan as at St Mary-at-Hill (page 22). The church was rebuilt according to Wren's original plans, thus giving it an 'authenticity' not found in any of the Wren churches which may have survived the Second World War undamaged. Such churches have many additional items, such as stained glass, which were not found in Wren's day.

The church was saved partly by the intrepidity of its vergeress, who kept it open after the war even when the City surveyor had served a dangerous structure notice. Seventeenth-century woodwork survives. Since its reconsecration in 1966, the church has been used by Lutheran congregations.

ST BARTHOLOMEW-THE-GREAT
pre-Great Fire.
SMITHFIELD

Rahere, a courtier of King Henry I, had a vision of St Bartholomew when returning from a pilgrimage to Rome. In the vision the apostle told him to found a priory on the Smooth Field (Smithfield), where the horse fairs were held outside the City wall. This he did in 1123 for Augustinian canons, with himself as the first prior. They made it their business to look after poor men and this was the beginning of St Bartholomew's Hospital, west of the church.

The priory was entered by the present 13th century porch, which has an Elizabethan-style timbered house above it. The priory nave extended the whole length of the present churchyard, and one side of its cloisters, much restored and rebuilt and early 15th-century in style, remains on the east side.

The brick tower, with its wooden turret and gilded vane, dates from the 17th century. In the tower are five medieval bells, the oldest complete ring in London. They are still regularly rung for Sunday services and weddings.

The porch and west front of flint

RIGHT: *The old brick tower of St Bartholomew-the-Less.*

and Portland stone are by Sir Aston Webb (1893); so are the north porch and other flint refacings of the church. The old red-brick verger's house, looking like a Cotman water-colour and a reminder of the East Anglian quality of the city, is built into the north wall of the church. It is the sole surviving relic of the brick buildings which were built into most of the priories after the Dissolution of the Monasteries during the reign of King Henry VIII.

At one time there was a printing works in the Lady Chapel where Benjamin Franklin worked and, until 1885, there was a fringe factory supported on iron columns above what is now the High Altar.

The interior is a contrast. It is the Norman choir of the priory with vaulted aisles and triforium and new-looking Lady Chapel of 1330, with a vaulted crypt below it, all sedulously restored by Sir Aston Webb in 1897. But the texture of the Norman part remains and the 1890 seats as in a monastic choir.

From the west end, looking east, there is a definite cathedral-like impression. The transepts are there with their arches and an attractive vista to the much restored stone-vaulted cloister. The font is medieval. Rahere's tomb, elegantly rebuilt under a canopy in about 1405 and much repainted lately, contrasts with the solid Norman pillars of the sanctuary on the north side of which it is placed. Opposite, in the triforium, a glazed window of about 1510 looks down on it. (This can be seen in the photograph on the inside front cover.)

The prettiest of the 17th-century monuments is the one to Elizabeth Freshwater, which shows a kneeling figure with angels at either side. Sir Walter Mildmay, founder of Emmanuel College Cambridge, has a monument here (1589).

LEFT: *St Anne and St Agnes was rebuilt to Wren's original plans after the Blitz and is now a Lutheran church.*

ST BARTHOLOMEW-THE-LESS
pre-Great Fire and 19th century.
SMITHFIELD

The small church, whose parish is the hospital, the 15th-century and medieval tower with newel stair turret and rough stone walls, can be seen from Smithfield Market. On the west and north sides of the church are signs of medieval walls and early brick.

The church is intriguing inside because of its ingenious octagonal shape devised by George Dance Junior (1789) and coarsened in the 19th century. The west end to the left of the entrance has its old floor and a brass.

The octagonal church glimpsed beyond has a groined and vaulted roof and clerestoried windows. Its walls are painted and lit by stained glass and lead patterning designed by Hugh Easton after the Second World War. The pews and fittings are mostly Victorian and were toned down by Lord Mottistone and Paul Paget in the post-war restoration. The walls are an album of monuments from the 17th century onwards.

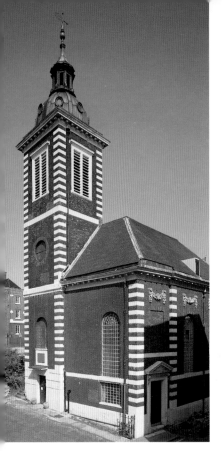

ABOVE: *The Dutch-looking exterior of St Benet, Paul's Wharf. Inside is one of the least spoiled City churches.*

ST BENET, PAUL'S WHARF

(also known as St Benet's Welsh Church)
Wren 1677–85.
QUEEN STREET

A Dutch-looking exterior with its dark red brick broad eaves, round-headed windows of clear glass and stone festoons and tall brick tower with stone quoins and little lead dome and steeple. It stands on a curving, cobbled hill and was used by ecclesiastical lawyers from the Doctors Commons and heralds from the College of Arms opposite who sat in the north aisle which has hipped roofs. Inside, it is one of the least spoiled City churches. The north and west galleries remain; the gallery fronts are carved with fruit. The bases of the columns which support the gallery are panelled. The columns themselves, which should be marbled, spring from the gallery height as they once did in St Bride's,

Fleet Street. The old stone floors survive with slate monuments. The pews, though cut down, are made from the wood of the original box pews. The pulpit is richly but roughly decorated. The grand west doorcase has cherubs and the Stuart arms above. The altar-piece with urns on top and broken pediments, Commandment boards, Creed and Paternoster and carved panels, dominates the church above an elaborate 17th-century altar table, inlaid on top and supported by baroque angels. There are many nice 18th-century monuments, particularly one designed to fit the south-east corner. The organ was rebuilt in 1979 in its original 1830 position in the West Gallery. The church was completely redecorated in the 1970s and regilded at a cost of £50,000; at the same time modern lighting was installed. The inlaid sounding board of the pulpit is in the roof of the porch. The church became the Metropolitan Welsh Church of the City and Diocese of London by Act of Parliament in 1879.

ST BOTOLPH, ALDERSGATE

rebuilt 1788, Nathanial Wright.
ALDERSGATE STREET

Outside, this church is a bleak, brown-brick oblong, with a western brick tower and pretty wooden turret and gilded vane. The east front was added in 1831 and has a Classical facade in olive and dark green. The large churchyard is laid out as an inoffensive garden.

The interior is an exalting contrast and is by Nathaniel Evans (1788), who was clearly influenced by George Dance Junior's interior to All Hallows London Wall. Panelled columns support wooden galleries over the north and south aisles. The columns are square to the gallery height and Corinthian above, marbled, and with gilded capitals. Round-headed windows, with gaudy stained glass, Victorian and 1940-ish, light the aisles. The barrel-vaulted roof has an elaborate plasterwork design of circles and central rosettes of leaves and flowers with hanging stamens. It is lit by a

clerestory of clear glass with simple, pretty leading. Semi-circular apse with half a dome above the altar, is painted blue and gold and dimly lit by a stained glass east window of brown and yellow, which appears between curtains moulded in plaster and coloured. The window, the only 18th-century transparency in the City, shows the Agony in the Garden, painted by John Pearson. The apse windows which flank it are hideously out of keeping, neo-primitive, post-war work. The fine organ case is in the right place over the delicate west gallery. The inlaid pulpit stands on a carved palm tree. Eighteenth-century and earlier monuments abound, as do swordrests, Victorian pews, altar rails, brown and yellow Victorian tiled floor. There is a deliberate contrast between the ornate, yellowish brown body of the church

ABOVE: *The pretty 18th-century tower and bell turret of St Botolph, Aldersgate.*

and the light, delicate clerestory and roof. In the north-east corner a tablet says:

> *Praises on tombs are trifles vainly spent.*
> *A man's good name is his best monument.*

RIGHT: *St Botolph, Aldgate houses several items from the 18th century, among them a beautiful font cover.*

ST BOTOLPH, ALDGATE

rebuilt 1741, George Dance the Elder.
ALDGATE HIGH STREET

A huge, dark brick church where the East End and City meet. It faces north and south and has a dumpy spire and stone quoins. The church is very much used and more a mission to the East End than a City church. The crypt is a rehabilitation centre for the homeless. Over the entrance door to the church above is a large royal arms and a view of the rich, dark, early Victorian east window. All the rest of the windows are releaded in pretty Classical patterns by J. F. Bentley (architect of Westminster Cathedral) who adorned the broad curved ceiling with a plaster design of angels and shields and put highly individual mouldings all over the ceilings and east wall. He also decorated the gallery fronts with balusters so that

the effect of the church is of advanced 1890 Classical in which may be seen handsome survivals of the 18th century, notably the domed font cover, like a little circular temple; the light, wrought iron Communion rails and inlaid pulpit; the organ case in the west gallery; and the altar-piece and Communion table. The batik hangings are a modern feature, designed in 1982 by Thetis Blacker on the theme 'Gate of Heaven' and covering three reredos panels.

ST BOTOLPH WITHOUT BISHOPSGATE

rebuilt 1725, James Gold.
BISHOPSGATE

It stands almost unencumbered by buildings in a grassy churchyard where there is a charming school of 1840, now a hall. The school is red brick Classic with niches containing statues of 18th-century children. The church is also of red brick with stone dressings and a stone tower ingeniously placed at the east end over the chancel. The west end is slightly recessed, which emphasises the double rows of windows in the nave. A drum-shaped glass dome was put on the nave roof in 1820. Inside, the church is a galleried oblong, all white and gold and brown and pale blue. There is much late Victorian decoration in the way of screens of wood and stained-glass, paintings in the chancel, leadwork in the lantern and carved choir stalls. Cachemaille-Day restored this church after the war so that it is lighter inside than it used to be. Pulpit, gallery fronts and Lady Chapel altar-piece are Georgian, as is the organ case (split in two to reveal a Hugh Easton version of the Ascension). The depth of the chancel

LEFT: *The light interior of St Botolph without Bishopsgate. Keats was baptised here in 1795.*

under the tower and massive mouldings add length and dignity to the church. The south-east chapel is the memorial chapel of the Honourable Artillery Company, and the London Rifle Brigade is remembered by a tablet in the south aisle and a book of remembrance below. Edward Alleyn, founder of Dulwich College, was baptised in the church in 1566, as was John Keats in 1795.

ST BRIDE'S, FLEET STREET
Wren 1670–84.
FLEET STREET

The Portland stone steeple of diminishing octagons, ending in a spirelet, like a ring of bells. Within its fanciful outline are shadows and openings, suited to the grey London sky. The tower and large, windowed oblong of the church below all harmonise. The church stands in a high churchyard and was originally designed to be seen above the Fleet River. Wren took trouble over the interior which, before the church was gutted in 1940, was magnificent, with galleries round three sides and the east window and altar-piece below it forming one composition. Pillars had double columns designed to support the galleries, which survived with the high pews. Mr Godfrey Allen has put in a composition of his own, arranging seats in the nave, college-chapel wise, bringing the east end forward with a Wren style altar-piece, into which is inserted a vesica of stained glass which does not look well in the woodwork.

Beyond, on the east wall, above the east window, a painting by Mr Glyn Jones ingeniously gives the impression that the wall is curved. The aisles behind the screens of the nave stalls are rather bleak. The barrel-vaulted nave ceiling and cross-vaulting over the aisles are as Wren designed them and gaily gilded. Glazing, except for the east end, is fortunately clear. Beneath the church are Roman and Saxon remains.

RIGHT: *The beautiful steeple of St Bride's, Fleet Street, which was designed by Wren.*

ST CLEMENT, EASTCHEAP
Wren 1683–7.
KING WILLIAM STREET

A modest little church which, from its unpretentiousness, is just the sort of place that gets destroyed by administrators. The plain tower, with quoins and balustrade, is not in the same plane as the pedimented west front, and is designed to be seen sideways on and to emphasise the curve of Clement's Lane. The churchyard at the back is a welcome oasis. The vestry occupies part of it.

Inside, the church is an oblong with a small south aisle, broader at the west end than at the east and separated from the nave by cast-iron columns. The windows are all clear glass, except for yellowish Victorian stained glass in the north clerestory.

The walls, originally white, are turning cream, but their plainness shows up the really splendid 17th-century pulpit with its huge canopy

RIGHT: *A view of the interior of St Clement, Eastcheap showing the splendid 17th-century pulpit.*

of wreaths and cherubs, and the panelling, doors and organ case at the west end.

The flat ceiling is enlivened by a huge plaster wreath of fruit and flowers set in an oblong panel. Butterfield's attempt (1872) to make this plain, classic oblong church into a Tractarian building is shown by the red and yellow tiled floors and raised choir and sanctuary, also tiled. The altar-piece has been painted gold and blue by Sir Ninian Comper (1933) so that it no longer harmonises with the pulpit and woodwork.

The 17th-century font and font cover remain as does an un-getatable carved cupboard for loaves. The walls all round are panelled. and there is a gilded swordrest.

standard; the font cover retains four of twelve gilded apostles. The font is surrounded by turned balusters. The altar-piece, with Moses and Aaron and wreaths and carved urns painted in gold, has panelling and doorcases either side of it; two high carved pews at the side of the south entrance; carved pulpit without sounding board. As usual, the box pews were chopped up to make choir stalls in Victorian times, when the sanctuary was created. Three of Wren's best churches – St Benet, Gracechurch Street, St Dionis, Backchurch, and All Hallows, Lombard Street – were destroyed and added to this parish.

ST DUNSTAN-IN-THE-WEST
John Shaw and John Shaw Jnr, 1831–3.
FLEET STREET

A brick octagon with a stone-faced tower and lantern and entrance porch on the south side. The tower dominates Fleet Street and the lantern, seen from Ludgate Circus, is well proportioned. The style of the whole church is an imitation of late Gothic, but the carved heads look Georgian. The clock, with wooden figures which strike bells in a wooden temple on the outside of the church, were originally on the old church when it jutted into Fleet Street, before Shaw's rebuilding on a site further back. The clock was rescued from St Dunstan's house in Regent's Park and returned here by the first Lord Rothermere. The statue of Queen Elizabeth over the schoolhouse entrance, and other statues there, were on Lud Gate before its demolition in 1760. Inside, this much-used and spacious vaulted octagon is big and surprising. The High Altar faces north. Pews, altars and a baptistry occupy six other sides. The 1831 nave pews, west gallery and organ case survived German bombing, when the central pendant and Gothic gasolier, designed by Shaw, were destroyed. The appropriate violent late-Geor-

gian stained glass was replaced after the war by watery modern stuff. Many monuments, some 17th-century, from the older church are on the walls.

ST EDMUND, KING AND MARTYR
Wren 1670–9.
LOMBARD STREET

Seen from Clement's Lane, the south and main front of this north/south-facing church is a handsome Portland stone composition, with long consoles. Wren added the octagonal lead spire (1706–7), the pedestals round which lack their gilded urns. Fund-raising is under way for the considerable sum needed to restore these urns to the brackets on the steeple. Inside, the impression is of Victorian restoration because of the east windows. The ceiling of the aisleless oblong nave comes to an abrupt end at the chancel and makes an awkward join with a semi-dome, painted in Victorian times, over the altar. The organ seems to have been divided in two. Part of one case is in the south gallery and the other on the west wall. The 17th-century woodwork in the church is of a high

RIGHT: *The stone-faced tower of St Dunstan-in-the-West dominates Fleet Street.*

THE CITY OF LONDON CHURCHES

This map shows the positions of existing churches (numerals), the towers remaining of demolished churches (letters). The site of nearly every lost City church is marked either by a graveyard or a tablet on a wall.

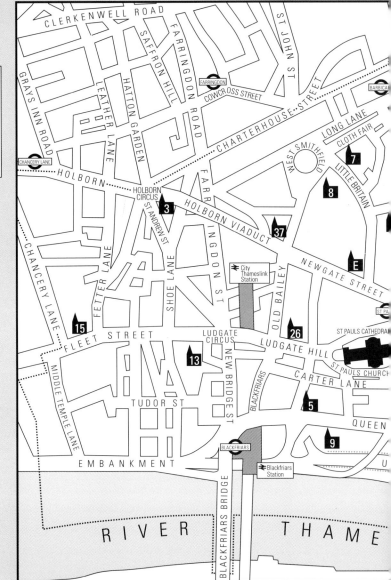

Existing Churches

1 All Hallows-by-the-Tower
2 All Hallows-on-the-Wall
3 St Andrew, Holborn
4 St Andrew Undershaft
5 St Andrew-by-the-Wardrobe
6 St Anne and St Agnes
7 St Bartholomew-the-Great
8 St Bartholomew-the-Less
9 St Benet, Paul's Wharf
10 St Botolph, Aldersgate
11 St Botolph, Aldgate
12 St Botolph without Bishopsgate
13 St Bride's, Fleet Street
14 St Clement, Eastcheap
15 St Dunstan-in-the-West
16 St Edmund, King and Martyr
17 St Ethelburga, Bishopsgate
18 St Giles', Cripplegate
19 St Helen's, Bishopsgate
20 St James, Garlickhythe
21 St Katherine Cree
22 St Lawrence Jewry
23 St Magnus the Martyr
24 St Margaret Lothbury
25 St Margaret Pattens
26 St Martin, Ludgate
27 St Mary Abchurch
28 St Mary Aldermary
29 St Mary-le-Bow
30 St Mary-at-Hill
31 St Mary Woolnoth
32 St Michael Cornhill
33 St Michael, Paternoster Royal
34 St Nicholas, Cole Abbey
35 St Olave, Hart Street
36 St Peter, Cornhill
37 St Sepulchre-without-Newgate
38 St Stephen Walbrook
39 St Vedast, Foster Lane

Tower Only Remaining

A All Hallows, Staining
B St Alban, Wood Street
C St Alphage, London Wall
D St Augustine-with-St Faith
E Christ Church, Newgate Street
F St Dunstan-in-the-East
G St Martin Orgar
H St Mary Somerset
J St Olave, Jewry

Destroyed in Great Fire and not Rebuilt

All Hallows, Honey Lane
All Hallows-the-Less
Holy Trinity-the-Less
St Andrew Hubbard
St Anne, Blackfriars
St Benet Sherehog
St Botolph, Billingsgate
St Faith-under-St Paul's
St Gabriel, Fenchurch
St John The Baptist-upon-Walbrook
St John The Evangelist
St John Zachary
St Lawrence, Pountney
St Leonard, Eastcheap
St Leonard, Foster Lane
St Margaret Moses
St Margaret, New Fish Street

St Martin Orgar
St Martin Pomeroy, or Iremonger
St Martin Vintry
St Mary Bothaw
St Mary Colechurch
St Mary Magdalen, Milk Street
St Mary Mounthaw
St Mary, Staining
St Mary Woolchurch
St Michael-le-Querne
St Nicholas Acon
St Nicholas Olave
St Olave, Silver Street
St Pancras, Soper Lane
St Peter, Paul's Wharf
St Peter, Westcheap
St Thomas the Apostle

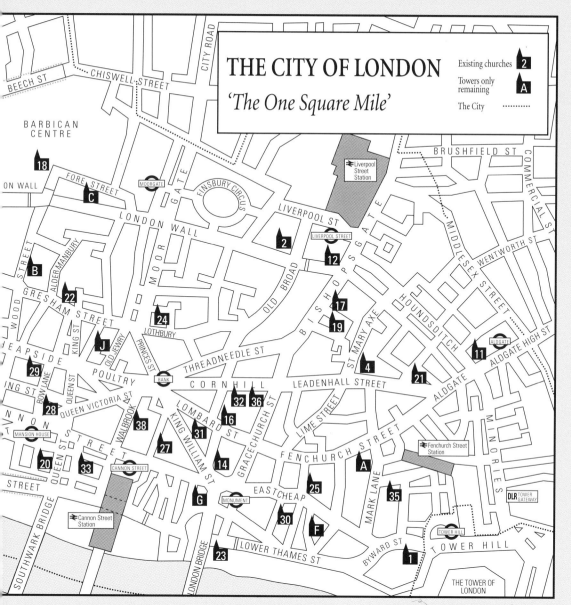

THE CITY OF LONDON
'The One Square Mile'

Existing churches **2**

Towers only remaining **A**

The City ············

Wren Churches Destroyed

All Hallows, Bread Street (sold 1894)
All Hallows-the-Great (sold 1894)
All Hallows, Lombard Street (sold 1938)
St Antholin, Watling Street (sold 1874)
St Bartholomew-by-the-Exchange
   (demolished 1891)
St Benet Fink (destroyed)
St Benet, Gracechurch Street (sold 1867)
St Christopher-le-Stocks (sold 1782)
St Dionis, Backchurch (sold 1878)
St George, Botolph Lane (sold 1901)
St Mary, Aldermanbury (bombed 1940,
   site sold, stones sent to USA)
St Mary Magdalen, Old Fish Street
   (sold 1887)
St Matthew, Friday Street (sold 1881)
St Michael Bassishaw (sold 1899)

St Michael, Crooked Lane (sold 1831)
St Michael, Queenhithe (sold 1875)
St Michael, Wood Street (sold 1897)
St Mildred, Bread Street
   (destroyed 1940, sold)
St Mildred, Poultry (sold 1872)
St Stephen, Coleman Street
   (bombed 1940, site sold)
St Swithin, London Stone
   (bombed 1940, sold c1960)

Other Churches Destroyed

Holy Trinity, Gough Square
   (1842 by J. Shaw; sold 1880)
Holy Trinity, Minories
   (1706, bombed 1940; sold)
St Catherine Coleman
   (1739, sold 1926)
St James, Duke's Place
   (post-Wren, sold 1874)
St Martin Outwich
   (1796, sold 1874)
St Peter-le-Poor
   (1792, sold 1907)
St-Thomas-in-the-Rolls
   (1842, sold 1882)

ST ETHELBURGA, BISHOPSGATE

pre-Great Fire and later.

BISHOPSGATE

Founded in 1250, St Ethelburga, the smallest of the City churches, suffered extensive damage from terrorist bombing in 1993. Only 51ft by 30ft in size, St Ethelburga was the best example of a City parish church of the Middle Ages, containing a magnificent reredos, woodcarving and wall monuments, most of which were damaged beyond repair. The church has now been rebuilt. It has a new function as a Centre for Reconciliation and Peace, hosting dialogue between those involved in national and international disputes. It also functions as an educational centre.

ST GILES', CRIPPLEGATE

pre-Great Fire and Victorian.

FORE STREET

The only church among the glassy slabs of the Barbican Scheme. A bastion of the City wall and a considerable length of the wall itself, which was revealed by the bombing, stretches southwards to the City. Outside, the church was, and still is, harshly repointed stone and mostly of Victorian date, except for a charming red-brick top stage of the tower with a white wooden turret above. This outline is the one familiar feature left in this part of the City landscape. Inside, devastating German bombing gave Godfrey Allen, the restorer, a free hand. Long north and south aisles are separated from the nave by a 15th-century arcade of seven bays. The windows, except those at the east and west ends which are new, are clear. The 18th-century organ from St Luke's, Old Street, is at the west end; a marble font with wooden cover and the pews

are from the same church. The roofs and panelling are new. Stone corbels recall the past, as do some stone arches in the painted monuments, canopied pulpit, sanctuary. John Milton's burial place is marked on a stone at the threshold of the chancel.

ST HELEN'S, BISHOPSGATE
pre-Great Fire.
BISHOPSGATE

St Helen's was badly damaged by a bomb which exploded in the City in 1992, and sustained further damage in the explosion which dev-astated St Ethelburga's in 1993. A programme has now been completed which has seen the repair to the roof, windows and glass, and the interior fittings, which include a table tomb. The 18th-century organ case has been dismantled, cleaned and put back in its original place on the gallery at the west end of the church. The re-ordered church opened again in 1996 with a level floor through-out, returning it to the pattern which existed between 1550 and 1893.

In the 14th century the north aisle belonged to a convent of Benedictine nuns who, in 1385, were reproved for 'the number of little dogs kept by the prioress, kissing secular persons and wearing osten-tatious veils . . .' As Wayland and Elizabeth Young go on to tell us, there were also 'waving over the screen which separated the parish nave from the convent nave, and too many children running about.' A 15th-century squint through which the nuns looked survives by the Easter Sepulchre at the east end of their nave. The main Victorian

LEFT: *A view of the nave of St Helen's, Bishopsgate, taken before the building was damaged by the terrorist bombs of 1992 and 1993. Unfortunately several City of London churches were affected by the 1993 bomb including St Ethelburga's, All Hallows-on-the-Wall, St Botolph without Bishopsgate and St Michael Cornhill.*

screen has been moved and placed between arches entering the south transept. The 17th century has a good showing in this big church in the painted monuments, canopied pulpit and wooden newel stair turret.

ST JAMES, GARLICKHYTHE
Wren 1676–82.
UPPER THAMES STREET

On a steep cobbled hill to the river a rough stone tower with elegant Port-land stone steeple (1714–17) rising from it, a variant on those of St Michael Paternoster Royal and St Stephen Walbrook. St James's steeple is three square temples with corner projections on the lower two. The church was bombed during the war and struck by a falling crane in 1991, but has since been sympathetically restored. It is greatly improved by having clear glass in round-headed windows and clerestoried roof, so as to justify the name of 'Wren's lantern'. It is the tallest City church interior. The columns are panelled to gallery height, and divide the church into nave and aisles. There is a west gallery with a fine organ case. The chancel has a painting of the Ascen-sion on the altar by Andrew Geddes. The vaulted ceiling is lit by the clerestory and a gilded oblong of plasterwork unites the chancel to the rich, dark organ case. Swordrests,

ironwork and carved wood abound; hat pegs on the churchwardens' pews and a wig stand on the pulpit, which came from St Michael Queenhithe (demolished 1874). Considering how bare this church looked after German bombing, it is a most skilful and sensitive restoration.

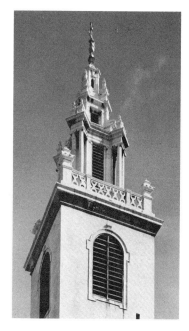

ABOVE AND BELOW: *The roof of St James, Garlickhythe was badly damaged by a falling crane in 1991 but has now been fully restored.*

ST KATHERINE CREE
pre-Great Fire.
LEADENHALL STREET

The City's pre-Fire attempt (1628–31) at the Renaissance. A hidden churchyard in the south-east corner with two plane trees and some table tombs and bushes. Embedded in the d'Avenon doorway is a memorial to James Fitch (who once had a cheese-mongers shop in the vicinity) which was erected by a descendant when the garden was restored in 1965. The outside walls of the church look Tudor, but there are Classic labels under the windows, a Classic porch and a splendid Renaissance sundial engraved on the south wall.

Inside the classical, composite columns are fortunately left free-standing and the effect of the nave with its low, new pews, Tudor clerestory and vaulting supported on round Classic arches with Gothic vaulted nave is a gay mixture of Gothic and Renaissance. The walls are white with mouldings picked out in grey and all bosses brightly painted. The square-headed east window has a Catherine wheel of

LEFT: *St Katherine Cree has a little dumpy stone tower (1504) which was vilely snail-pointed in the 19th century.*

cheerful 1830-ish glass, some of it older. The glass in the lower lights has disappeared and been bricked in. Unsympathetic pale green and blue Victorian glass remains in most of the windows, but some windows have roundels of 17th-century glass. The organ is of 1686 (Father Smith: rebuilt by Henry Willis in the 19th century); it was played on by Purcell, Handel and Wesley. The organ case and west gallery and doorcase in north-east corner are rich post-Fire carved woodwork, as are the pulpit and altar-piece. There are several monuments, notably the Throck-morton effigy (1571) and, strangely enough, a large model liner, reminding us of Lloyds of London.

ST LAWRENCE JEWRY
Wren 1670–87.
GRESHAM STREET

Very municipal, very splendid – the Corporation church. East wall at entrance to Guildhall square, with its pilasters and alcoves, is noble from either a sharp angle or straight-on view. The tower and west front were not designed to be exposed, as they now are, to public gaze. They were intended to be seen above the houses. The tower is at one angle, its

bell turret at another. The church was completely gutted by the Germans and the vestry, which had the richest plasterwork in the city, was destroyed. The restoration by Cecil Brown is all of a piece. The church consists of a double cube for nave, clerestoried and with round-headed windows and flat ceiling with plasterwork. To this a north aisle, lower than the nave, is joined, Corinthian pillars supporting the division. The vicarage is built into the north-west corner of the church over the vestry. The west gallery has a grand organ case. A wooden screen, with balustrade above, and wrought iron gates presented by the Royal Marines, the Parachute Regiment and the Airborne Forces, cuts off the north aisle. There are carved pews and organ case in the north aisle as well as nave. The panelled walls and altar-piece and carved woodwork generally seem very dark by contrast with the white walls and stone pilasters and light flat ceiling. The new stained glass is not really suited to a Wren church. Eight twinkling brass chandeliers light the nave and another the north aisle. The Royal Arms and those of the City of London look down on all.

BELOW: *St Lawrence Jewry. The nave is formed of a double cube with a clerestory and plasterwork ceiling.*

ST MARGARET LOTHBURY
Wren 1686–1700.
LOTHBURY

A white Portland stone church with corner tower and a lead steeple which is a variant on that of St Mary Abchurch, overshadowed by the bulk of the Bank of England.

Inside, the church gives a rich impression of elaborately carved dark woodwork, many brass candelabra, white and gold walls, all presided over by a west gallery and organ case at one end and a huge Flemish-looking screen across the east end. This screen came from All Hallows-the-Great when that Wren church was sold and demolished in 1894. The nave is an irregular parallelogram, with a carved altar-piece, brought back to its Renaissance splendour by Rodney Tatchell since the war and flanked by paintings of Moses and Aaron from St Christopher-le-Stocks (dem. 1781). The south aisle has the altar-piece from St Olave Jewry (dem. 1888, except for the tower) and monuments, too high up to see, from that church. Here too is St Margaret's marble font, whose sides are carved with scriptural subjects in relief in the homely manner of a 17th-century engraving.

ST MAGNUS THE MARTYR
Wren 1671–87.
LOWER THAMES STREET

The grand Portland stone tower with its octagonal lantern surmounted by a lead dome and spirelet and clock was Wren's welcome to the City for people coming over old London Bridge before the new bridge was built in 1831. The tower acted as a portico to the church and stood over the footway. The church is now partly hidden by the insolent neo-Egyptian bulk of Adelaide House. The north wall on Thames Street has a row of circular windows and sculptured panels and swags, rich for a City church exterior. Double gallery stairs with turned balusters, panelled Corinthian columns and glass screen form the entrance to a richly furnished interior: 'Inexplicable splendour of Ionian white and gold . . .' (Eliot). Tall, fluted Ionic columns support a barrel-vaulted nave and

ABOVE: *St Magnus the Martyr has a richly-furnished interior.*

ceiling lit by oval clerestory windows, fortunately with clear glass. High pews were cut down when Martin Travers restored the church in the full baroque of Anglo-Catholic Congress style of the 1920s. On top of the splendid altar-piece, with its Moses and Aaron and cherubs, he added a rood and devised baroque altars either side of it out of doorcases and displayed the wrought iron Communion rails to advantage. His low curving pews enable one to see the carved pulpit and enormous sounding board. Swordrests, ironwork, candle brackets and shrines abound. The walls are wood-panelled.

Unfortunately, since the Travers restoration, too much stained glass, unsuited to all Wren churches, has been introduced.

ST MARGARET PATTENS
Wren 1684.
EASTCHEAP

The tall lead spire and gilded vane still dominate several City views, especially from Aldgate and from St Mary-at-Hill opposite. The tower and church below are of Portland stone, which contrasts happily with the Georgian stucco house and shop front in a forecourt by the south entrance.

The church inside is a clerestoried oblong with a west gallery and north aisle. The north gallery is rather harshly blocked in for offices. The churchwardens' high pews under the west gallery have carved canopies and crown glass lunettes.

BELOW: *The spire of St Margaret Pattens in Eastcheap still dominates several views in the City.*

The walls of the church have been recently colourwashed. The capitals are gilded and they contrast well with the dark, old woodwork, wainscotting, swordrests, pulpit and carved woodwork converted into choir stalls. There are pretty 18th-century monuments, some of them curved round columns, and a marble font with cherubs. The parquet floors and cheap glass and yellow cross in east window, all postwar, spoil a charming interior.

ST MARTIN, LUDGATE
Wren 1677–87.
LUDGATE HILL

This church was one of Wren's later rebuildings and its lead spire is most carefully considered in relation to St Paul's. There is a point down Fleet Street where it exactly cuts the middle of the dome. Again, this spire may be seen over housetops, with its little balcony, from the lane opposite, near Apothecaries Hall, just as Wren intended his spires to be seen above the houses. This is one of the last such views left in the City. The Portland stone front has strongly marked cornices (consoles curl up the tower with a smaller pair on the final stone stage leading the eye up to the lead spire). It is a front designed to be seen sideways on. The interior is no anti-climax. Three thick arches with plaster coffers separate the Ludgate Hill front from the body of the

church and between them is a screen with carved doorcases and a gallery above. This screen was designed to keep off the noise of Ludgate Hill. The interior is tall and cruciform. Four columns, panelled even higher than former box pews, support the crossing, barrel-vaulted transepts, nave and chancel. From the middle hangs a chandelier. The plasterwork cornices end abruptly at the ends of the transepts, nave and west gallery. The old floors remain, except that the sanctuary and chancel were raised in Victorian times. The church is darkened by greenish, sub-Kempe style glass. Altar-piece, altar table, rails, pulpit, west gallery, organ case, font cover and lectern, two-seated chair and entrance doorcases on south and north walls are all 17th-century. North of the church are a churchyard and vestry. The west wall is part of the medieval city wall.

LEFT: *The church of St Martin, Ludgate was one of Wren's later rebuildings, and designed to be seen sideways on.*

ST MARY ABCHURCH
Wren 1681–7.
CANNON STREET

A square building of pale red 17th-century London brick with stone dressings, tower and lead spire. The tower is best seen from Sherborne Lane. The churchyard on the south front is cobbled in patterns. The interior is a complete surprise. This, with its painted dome, clear windows, wealth of carved woodwork, panelled pews and carved west gallery front and doorcases, 18th-century monuments and swordrests, is certainly one of the most beautiful in the City. It is both uplifting and intimate and, although it has the appearance of regularity, with pendentives under the dome, when you start to look, no side is quite the same. There are three levels of attraction: ground and eye level, with dark woodwork and old stone for floors; wall level, with the shadows of the vaulting under the dome and the white spaces cut into by the sounding board, exceptionally rich

LEFT: *St Mary Abchurch. The interior is a complete surprise and one of the most beautiful in the City.*

monuments and urns, dominated by the grand altar-piece with genuine Grinling Gibbons' carving; and then roof level, with its painted dome in home-made looking perspective, lit by oval lunettes, showing angels round the Glory, and a cornice with swags and shells and figures all by William Snow, a local painter-stainer. The painting was well-restored after the blitz by Hoyle. Godfrey Allen was the architect of the sensitive restoration of the fabric, after Hitler destroyed the Victorian glass and tiled floor. Panelled box pews are round three sides: font and cover are in a railed enclosure.

ST MARY ALDERMARY
Wren 1682; tower 1701.
QUEEN VICTORIA STREET

A prominent church at the traffic intersection by Mansion House Underground station. It is ashlar-faced outside and Gothic through-out. Wren rebuilt the upper stage of the old tower, which survived the Fire, to fit in with the Gothic interior he had already designed.

Inside, the plan is medieval with north and south aisles. The east wall is not square to the chancel as the old east wall was retained. The aisles are charmingly roofed by Wren (unusually, all in plaster) in his own version of late Perpendicular fan-vaulting. This consists of circular saucer domes and semi-circles with the spaces in between filled with quatrefoil panelling.

The clerestoried nave has a Gothic panelled ceiling rising from pretty baroque corbels between the Perpendicular-style arcaded columns of the nave. There is a wooden swordrest. The pulpit, font and font cover survive from the 17th century. In 1876 all the rest of the Wren furnishings were removed in a heavy-handed effort to make the interior what was then thought to be truly medieval.

BELOW: *The fat pinnacles of the tall thin tower of St Mary Aldermary are tipped with golden fibreglass finials.*

ST MARY-LE-BOW

(also known as Bow Church)
Wren 1670–83, rebuilt 20th century.
CHEAPSIDE

The tower and steeple are by Wren. The body of the church was probably not by Wren and is now, since the church was gutted in 1941, largely by Laurence King. The scale is very grand, though the detail is less intricate and homely than in a Wren church. The High Altar is arranged for a westward position with the Bishop's Throne at the east end behind it. The steepled Sacrament house is in the south-east chapel. The broad, curved ceiling is divided into coloured panels. A modern rood hangs to make the division between nave and chancel.

RIGHT: *An interior view of St Mary-le-Bow. This church was rebuilt by Laurence King in 1964.*

LEFT: *The tower and steeple of St Mary-le-Bow are by Wren. The body of the church has been rebuilt.*

The new east windows are by John Hayward of stained glass and in a modern style. The prevailing colours in the church are white and gold with green and pale blue in the ceiling. There are black and white stone floors, and low wooden panelling round the walls. Under the church is a three-aisled Norman crypt (*c.*1090) with cushion capitals. In part of the crypt the Court of Arches is held for deciding Ecclesiastical Law cases and for confirming the election of bishops. The whole crypt is a pleasant amalgam of slate-and-stone floors, old brick and stone and modern concrete supports. It is a marked contrast with the vast church above.

ST MARY-AT-HILL

Wren 1670–6; tower 1780; interior partly rebuilt by James Savage, 1843.
EASTCHEAP

Sadly this church was burnt down but has been rebuilt, though the fittings inside have still to be restored. It was the least spoiled and the most gorgeous interior in the City, all the more exciting by being hidden away among cobbled alleys, paved passages and brick walls overhung by a plane tree. From the east wall projects a clock over St Mary-at-Hill. The entrance under the west tower is from Lovat Lane. There is a churchyard on the north side and a rectory on the south on the other side of a brick passage. The plasterwork was in an Adam style later than Wren, but delicate and an airy contrast with the massive and splendid woodwork with which the church abounds. The west end, with its glass and wood screen, gallery and magnificent organ case, the high pews with their many delicate swordrests, the altar-piece, altar table, turned Communion rails, the sounding board and pulpit below, approached by a long wooden staircase with carved balusters, were all seen in a mysterious light filtering through windows of clear glass with a few pretty early Victorian bands of colour. The atmosphere of merchant grandeur, pew-openers and the time of Dickens was unforgettable. Much of the carving and repair work carried out by W. Gibbs Rogers in the 1840s,

churchyard. Inside, he left a legacy in the form of angels supporting the ceiling, carved Victorian pew ends by Gibbs Rogers, of the most expensive sort with doors, Lombardised pulpit and marble east end. There is an enormous wooden pelican (1775) at the west end, feeding its young. The organ looks awkward in the north-east corner. There are modest 17th-century monuments on walls and a wrought iron swordrest.

Victorian glass, which reduced the church to an unlit cavern, has been lightened and the clerestory shows Wren's pretty cross-vaulted aisles have ceiling lunettes. From the churchyard, Scott's Lombardising of Wren's windows is particularly evident. Hawksmoor gave this once Classic church a Gothic pinnacled tower of Portland stone, having no objection to a blend of styles. It must have been this tower which gave Scott the idea of trying to make Wren's Classical church Gothic and Lombardic.

again after a fire, was so good that it was hard to make out which was 17th-century and which was Gibbs Rogers.

ST MARY WOOLNOTH
Hawksmoor 1716–27.
LOMBARD STREET

A sumptuous and prominent church, differing markedly from the curves and lightness of Wren. Hawksmoor, his highly original pupil, uses mathematical regularity, squareness and weight in this, his only church in the City. The north wall and twin towers were originally the only parts exposed and, with their strong rustications, they show how to make blank walls interesting. Outside, the south wall is obscured by a vestry block, *c.*1900, but the north and west fronts are seen as Hawksmoor designed them. Inside, the church resolves itself into a pilastered square with four clear-glass windows on one side, with a higher interior square marked off by four groups of three fluted columns supporting frieze, beam and strong cornice, above which are four big clerestory semi-circular windows, enhancing the ceiling, typical of Hawksmoor

ABOVE: *Wren's highly original pupil Hawksmoor was the architect of St Mary Woolnoth.*

with its heavy plaster moulding set in from the cornice. On the east side, dimpled cherubs support a royal coat of arms. The Roman baroque carved oak reredos, inlaid pulpit and sounding board were designed by Hawksmoor. Butterfield made alterations (1875) removing the galleries and pushing back their fronts and the organ case to the walls. His paved floor scheme, enriched as the altar is approached, survives.

ST MICHAEL, CORNHILL
Wren 1669–72. Tower by Hawksmoor 1718–24.
CORNHILL

Despite modern efforts to tone it down and make the interior cheerful, nothing can de-Victorianise this Wren church. Sir George Gilbert Scott added the richly carved porch on Cornhill and the vaulted cloister on the south side leading to the

RIGHT: *The pinnacled tower of St Michael, Cornhill, was also designed by Hawksmoor.*

porting a vane. St Michael's is now restored and the west gallery and western part of the church is used for offices. The nave is very much as it was since before the war, except for an unfortunate deep blue paint in the ceiling, and some up to date stained glass in the east windows of the nave.

ST NICHOLAS, COLE ABBEY
Wren 1671–81.
QUEEN VICTORIA STREET

The lead spire, like an inverted trumpet, is surmounted by a gilded ship from the Wren church of St Michael Queenhithe, demolished 1875. St Nicholas was gutted in 1941. Its exterior south wall of Portland stone, the range of clear glass, round-headed windows on the north and south, are more seen than they were before the war, when the church was hidden by buildings. Inside, it is a plain room with a west gallery and screen under three arches. The flat ceiling is divided into panels. The capitals of the pilasters on the walls and the swags over the east window are round-headed and far apart. The stained glass artist, Keith New, has

ABOVE: *The church of St Michael, Paternoster Royal, where Dick Whittington, once Lord Mayor of London, is buried.*
BELOW: *Dick Whittington and his cat depicted in stained glass.*

ST MICHAEL PATERNOSTER ROYAL
Wren 1686–94.
COLLEGE STREET

The church is now prominent. It used to be hidden down the narrow Thamesbank slope of College Hill on which still stand the baroque 17th-century doors of the College next to the church, founded by Dick Whittington, who is buried in St Michael's. German bombing between the church and Thames opened a view of the stone south wall of the tower and steeple. The best view is still that looking west from outside the Innholders' Hall in the turn off Dowgate Hill (where there is a clutch of old Livery Company halls). Here one sees the old red-brick walls and east end of the church with stone cherubs, and the stone-faced tower beyond. St Michael's steeple is a round colonnaded temple with round urns on it, a middle stage with curving corbels, more urns and round turret sup-

BELOW: *The lead spire of St Nicholas, Cole Abbey.*

ABOVE: *There is a monument to Samuel Pepys, the diarist, in the church of St Olave, Hart Street.*

tried to make a horizontal composition of them with a design suggesting a long ship. All the woodwork is Renaissance; some of it is original, but it is so very much cleaned and light that it all looks new. There are pulpit, font cover, panelled walls, Royal Arms and swordrest. The building is now a national centre for religious education.

ST OLAVE, HART STREET
pre-Great Fire.
FENCHURCH STREET

A country church in the world of Seething Lane. The churchyard on the south side, entered under a gate with a skull and crossbones, is a real churchyard and not got up as a Garden of Rest. The church survived the Great Fire, was three parts demolished by bombs in 1941 but restored in its original style by Ernest Glanfield. It has a ragstone tower and walls. The tower has brick 17th-century top stage and lantern, rather like St Giles' Cripplegate, and with a projecting clock. The vestry house looks on to the churchyard. Inside, the vestry has a humble plaster ceiling with cheerful cherubs. The entry

from Hart Street is by three steep, sudden steps down. The small clerestoried church has north and south aisles of three bays. Gaily coloured 17th-century monuments deck the walls and clasp the easternmost columns of the sanctuary. They vie in this whitewashed interior with patches of modern stained glass whose general effect is good. Notable among the monuments are those to Samuel Pepys and his wife Elizabeth, who are buried here together. There are a 17th-century carved pulpit, four swordrests, 17th-century Communion rails, new wooden roofs, stone floors, oak benches and a new west screen and gallery by Glanfield. Under the tower, steps go down to a well and a small and plain stone vaulted crypt.

RIGHT: *The tower of St Peter, Cornhill is surmounted by a green copper dome and spirelet bearing St Peter's keys.*

ST PETER, CORNHILL
Wren 1667–87.
CORNHILL

Still surrounded by shops, as most City churches used to be. The crazy-paved churchyard on the south side gives a view of stucco south wall and pretty dark red brick tower.

You enter under the organ gallery and notice four rich doorcases at the west end and hear the ticking clock in the gallery below the organ case with gilded pipes. An effect of carved woodwork prevails. Square panelled columns divide the church into nave and aisles, ingeniously arranged into double heights. The walls are panelled to the height of the window sills. Across the east end is a classic screen with lion and unicorn on top. The pulpit has a richly adorned sounding board and stairs.

The Victorian pews and pew platforms have been removed and a tiled floor laid, with chairs for seating. The painting above the Communion Table and the eight windows above it are Victorian. Despite the glass, Victorian and modern, this is a most attractive interior now it has been cleaned and whitened. The marble font and its wooden, carved cover are in the south-east corner.

ST SEPULCHRE-WITHOUT-NEWGATE
(properly the church of the Holy Sepulchre)
pre-Fire and subsequent centuries.
HOLBORN VIADUCT

This is the biggest parish church in the City and has associations with Old Bailey opposite. The handbell which rang in condemned prisoners' ears the night before execution and the rhyming admonitions shouted to the poor wretches are in the church. The tenor bell in the tower tolled them to their deaths at eight in the morning.

The nave aisles are faced with Portland stone outside and with a charming 17th-century sundial on the south aisle parapet.

The two-storeyed south porch and the tower itself were refaced externally in the 1870s so as to look

BELOW: *The nave of St Sepulchre-without-Newgate, the largest parish church in the City, is a forest of tall pillars. The bell of St Sepulchre tolled condemned prisoners to their deaths.*

old, but their effect is Victorian. You enter by the 15th-century fan-vaulted porch to a forest of tall pillars. There are north and south aisles and a further chapel to the north, dedicated to musicians.

Despite its noble proportions and vaulted plaster ceilings of 1834 and curved monuments on the columns, the effect of the interior is muddled because things have unfortunately been shifted from their right places.

The Renatus Harris organ case, with its gilded cherubs and pipes, is one of the most beautiful in the city and has been moved from the west gallery to the north aisle. The twin pulpits were made in 1854 but have been cut down in height. The 17th-century woodwork has been Lombardised by the Victorians. Screens, ancient and modern, abound, as do flags, and swordrests. There are pale, newish stained glass windows. The High Altar is set forward. There is a very pretty octagonal font cover dating from 1670 with cherubs and Royal Arms.

ST STEPHEN WALBROOK
Wren 1672–7.
WALBROOK

The dome of this church was designed by Wren before that of St Paul's. Some pretty views of its green copper exterior and lantern can be glimpsed between buildings. The west tower is of ragstone with Portland stone steeple (1717), a separate composition standing above the street which was once a stream – the Walbrook. The church is entered at the west, through a baroque screen under an organ case with the Stuart Royal Arms. A colonnade effect is given by the sixteen columns, twelve of which support the dome, whose coffered decoration is broken by a band of wreaths. Under the dome is an additional altar of Roman travertine sculpted by Henry Moore, round which are circles of beechwood benches carved by Andrew Varah. The contemporary pulpit,

BELOW: *St Stephen Walbrook, where Wren has shown how to make a plain rectangle interesting and full of vistas.*

ABOVE: *The white stone tower of St Vedast supports Wren's most subtle steeple, which was designed to contrast with that of St Mary-le-Bow nearby.*
ABOVE RIGHT: *The interior of St Vedast.*

altar rails, altar and altar-piece, font and font cover survive, as does the baptistry screen made from Thomas Colley's Victorian choir stalls. Light comes from oval windows, round-headed west windows and a clerestory which shows up rich and attractively rough plasterwork. Lodovico Cardi's *Adoration of the Magi* hangs over the vestry door. The best way to enjoy the spacious interior is to see how the grouping of columns changes as one walks round. Sir John Vanbrugh and John Dunstable are buried here. In 1953 The Samaritans was founded (to befriend the suicidal and despairing) in the vestries. The organisation is now worldwide. The original telephone, the world's first 'hot line', is on a plinth in the south-west corner of the church.

ST VEDAST-ALIAS-FOSTER
Wren 1695–1700.
CHEAPSIDE

This Portland stone oblong church is built on medieval remains and there is still a curving wall of the old stone and brick at the south-west corner. The adjacent rectory, with a pretty colonnaded cloister, is by Stephen Dykes-Bower, who restored the church after German bombing. The white stone tower supports Wren's subtlest steeple, designed to contrast, in its simplicity, with the elaborate steeple of St Mary-le-Bow nearby. Above the tower, the steeple starts as a concave-sided turret, it then supports a smaller convex turret topped by an obelisk and vane. Both turrets have wide openings so that from some angles it appears hollow and from others solid. Post-war building has almost obliterated the magical changes of this steeple.

Inside, the church is now a plain oblong, fitted with facing seats like a college chapel. The south aisle is a side chapel, cut off by an arcade of pillars and the high screen formed by

the backs of the south stalls. The church is lit by clear-glass round-headed windows and a clerestory. The east window has stained glass by Brian Thomas in brown and yellow, designed to fit in with a Clayton and Bell window which survived the bombing. The ceiling is flat with an oblong plaster wreath enclosing gilded rectangles and two elaborate wreaths of leaves and flowers, painted with silver aluminium and gilt. The floor is black and white; the woodwork is toned down. A grand 17th-century carved organ case from St Bartholomew-by-Exchange is in the west gallery, and the carved font and cover are from St Anne and St Agnes. The octagonal pulpit with a rich design of fruit and flowers, lions and skulls, is from All Hallows, Bread Street (demolished in 1878). Below the west gallery, the small semi-circular windows at the top of the screen support plaster cherubs. The wooden altar-piece is from St Christopher-le-Stocks (demolished in 1781). There are a swordrest and Royal Arms.

Towers only

ALL HALLOWS, STAINING
MARK LANE

The 15th-century stone battlemented tower, vilely snail-pointed, stands like a bit of stage scenery beside a brick church hall in a well of new offices near Fenchurch Street Station. From inside the tower, steps go down to a vaulted crypt with carved ribs of Transitional Norman date (*c.* 1300) originally at Cripplegate, then in Islington and piously removed here in 1873. The body of All Hallows church (1671) was demolished in 1870.

ST ALBAN, WOOD STREET
WOOD STREET

The medieval church was rebuilt by Wren in Gothic (1682–7) and heavily Victorianised by Gilbert Scott in 1858, and gutted in 1940. The tower is by Wren (1697–8) but the top stage and pinnacles are Victorian.

ST ALPHAGE, LONDON WALL
LONDON WALL

The plain Classic church, rebuilt 1777, was demolished in 1924, with a Perpendicular style porch of 1914. The rubble, carefully preserved like a museum piece below the elevated pavement, is the remains of the 14th-century part of the church.

ST AUGUSTINE-WITH-ST FAITH
WATLING STREET

The oblong Wren church (1680–87) was destroyed in 1941 and has become part of the St Paul's Choir School on this site. The stone tower, with its corner obelisks and pierced parapet, was suffered to remain. The lead steeple (1695–8) which Wren designed and was an elongated onion, was carefully related to St Paul's, with whose massiveness it formed a light contrast, and was matched on the other side of the Cathedral by the spire of St Martin, Ludgate (page 20). The steeple was rebuilt after its collapse in the 19th century in a less interesting form. It was destroyed by bombs in the war, and then rebuilt in glass fibre to Wren's original design.

CHRIST CHURCH, NEWGATE STREET
NEWGATE STREET

This was one of Wren's most expensive churches and was built on the chancel site of the Franciscan Greyfriars church between 1677 and 1691. The body was huge and splendid and used by the Bluecoat boys whose school, Christ's Hospital, stood here till 1902. The church was gutted in 1940 and was not rebuilt, the ruins and cemetery now a garden. The tower and steeple are also by Wren (1703–4). The original splendour of the diminishing square turrets was restored by the late Lord Mottistone in 1960, who appealed in the *Daily Telegraph* for money to put back the numerous stone urns (many removed in the early 19th century) and received it from a lady in Leicester.

LEFT: *Christ Church, Newgate Street was gutted in 1940.*
RIGHT: *St Dunstan-in-the-East.*

Acknowledgements

All photographs were taken by Newbery Smith Photography, London and are © Pitkin Publishing Ltd, except for the following:
A.R. Marshall: title page; The Royal Society: p.4; Mary Evans Picture Library: p.5; St Michael Paternoster Church: p.24 top, bottom left; Angelo Hornak: p.26 left; Mark Fiennes: p.26 right.
Pitkin Guides would also like to thank the vicars of the churches mentioned in the text for their help in updating this edition.

City of London map on pages 14 and 15 revised and updated by The Map Studio Ltd, Romsey, 2003.

Edited by Ann Lockhart.
Designed by John Buckley.

Publication in this form © Pitkin Publishing Ltd 1993, latest reprint 2007.

Printed in Great Britain.
ISBN 978 0 85372 565 7

6/07